Bonjour, Piano!

ISBN 978-1-4950-8866-7

DURAND SALABERT ESCHIG
Editions Musicales

Visit Hal Leonard Online at
www.halleonard.com

CONTENTS

Editorial suggestions in the music appear in brackets.

COMPOSER BIOGRAPHIES

MÉLANIE "MEL" BONIS
(1858-1937)

Mélanie Bonis was born into a Parisian lower middle-class family of strong Catholic morals. Despite the child showing early signs of musical talent, her parents only agreed to let her study music after a recommendation from a friend who was professor of cornet at the Conservatoire. At age 16, she met César Franck, who gave her piano lessons. In a singing class, she developed a close relationship with Amédée Landély Hettich, a singing student and poet, and began setting his poems to music. Mélanie's parents strongly disapproved of her romance with Hettich. They forced her out of the Conservatoire and arranged a marriage for her in 1883 to Albert Domange, a businessman with no real affinity for music. Eventually Mélanie began meeting with Hettich again as an outlet for new composition and returning to the music scene. Their reunion eventually led to an illegitimate child, who she had to hide for much of her life. In the following years she put all her energy into her music and became a member of the SCM (Société des compositeurs de musique). She received performances of her music by some of the finest musicians of the time, and composed about three hundred works in all, though few were published. She used the name "Mel" because women composers were viewed disparagingly in her era.

OLIVIER HAURAY
(b. 1952)

Olivier Hauray was trained in organ and piano at the Caen Conservatory and with private teachers, and studied musicology at the Sorbonne. His career has been dedicated entirely to teaching piano; *Introduction to the piano by styles* volumes 1 and 2 are the result of his experiences as pedagogue confronted with the difficulties that student pianists have to solve. The books contain Hauray's original pedagogical pieces, emulating musical styles from Baroque to jazz, and proposing the technical solutions for their expressive purpose. Olivier Hauray continues to compose according to his musical encounters and his educational projects.

ERIK SATIE
(1866-1925)

One of the most eccentric personalities in all of music, Satie began piano studies in 1874, with a teacher who instilled a love of medieval music and chant. He entered the Paris Conservatoire in 1878, and was expelled two and a half years later for lack of talent. He was readmitted in 1885, but did not change the minds of his professors. After a detour in the Infantry – seen for a moment as a better career choice – Satie settled in the artistic Paris neighborhood of Montmartre in 1887. There he composed his first pieces: *Ogives*, for piano, written without barlines (a compositional choice found frequently in Satie's music) and the famous *Gymnopédies*. In 1890, while pianist and conductor at the cabaret Le Chat Noir, he met Claude Debussy and joined the spiritual movement Rose-Croix du Sâr Péladan (Rosicrucian Order), eventually becoming a choirmaster for the group. His involvement inspired the works *Sonneries de la Rose+Croix* and *Le Fils des Etoiles*. He had a brief and passionate relationship with the painter Suzanne Valadon in 1893. Brokenhearted after Suzanne left, he wrote *Vexations*, a theme to be played 840 times in a row – about twenty hours. In 1895 Satie abandoned his usual red robe and replaced it with seven identical mustard velvet suits, nicknaming himself "the Velvet Gentleman." In the next few years he moved to the suburb of Arcueil, and began taking composition lessons at the Schola Cantorum. He met Jean Cocteau, with whom he collaborated on the ballet *Parade* in 1916. Satie gradually met more artists of the French avant-garde, and presided over the birth of the group "Les Six." He died in 1925 of cirrhosis of the liver – probably due to his abundant consumption of absinthe. His friends visited his room in Arcueil – to which he had denied access throughout his life – and they discovered the state of poverty in which Satie had always lived.

ALEXANDRE TANSMAN
(1897-1986)

Tansman was born in Łódź, Poland, but lived in France for most of his life. While in Poland he trained in music at the Łódź Conservatory and completed a doctorate in law at the University of Warsaw (1918). After moving to Paris in 1920, he met Stravinsky and Ravel, both of whom encouraged his work. Tansman found his way into the École de Paris, a group of foreign musicians that included Bohuslav Martinů. Tansman enjoyed international success, with his orchestral music performed under such esteemed conductors as Koussevitzky, Toscanini, and Stokowski. During an American concert tour as pianist with Koussevitzky and the Boston Symphony in 1927, Tansman met George Gershwin. His concertizing also took him to Europe, Asia, Palestine and India, where he was a guest of Mahatma Gandhi in 1933. He gained French citizenship in 1938, but because of his Jewish heritage, he and his family were soon forced to flee France to the United States. Settled in Los Angeles, Tansman became acquainted with Schoenberg and composed a number of film scores. He returned to Paris in 1946. His honors included the Coolidge Medal (1941), election to the Académie Royale of Belgium (1977) and the Polish Medal of Cultural Merit (1983). He composed hundreds of pieces in total, exploring practically every musical genre, from symphonies to ballets to chamber music and works for solo guitar.

POINTS FOR PRACTICE AND TEACHING

Little Prelude to the Day / *Petit Prélude à la journée*
from Picturesque Child's Play / *Enfantillages pittoresques*
Erik Satie

- Both hands remain in five-finger position throughout, with no crosses or hand position changes.
- Though it may look like there are a lot of notes on these two pages, know that once you learn m. 1-16, you've learned m. 33-48; they are exactly the same!
- Notice how in m. 17-24, the R.H. plays eighth note figures while the L.H. plays half notes. Then in m. 25-32 the R.H. has the half notes and the L.H. has eighths.
- In every two-note slur, lean into the first note and don't accent the second.
- Pass evenly between the hands with steady eighth notes.
- Satie only gave one dynamic at the very beginning of the piece, so work on shaping the music in your own way.

Melodies in Octaves / *Deux Mélodies à l'Unisson No. 1*
Olivier Hauray

- These two short sections explore different articulations.
- The first melody has some tenuto markings, meaning to hold the note for its full value and emphasize it.
- Note the octave leap in m. 4 in both hands.
- In m. 5-8, the hands move to new positions for each phrase. Practice each hand separately and slowly.
- The second melody alternates between *staccato* and *legato* articulation.
- The hands stay in five-finger position, though the fourth finger of the R.H. and the second finger of the L.H. play both F natural and F-sharp.
- This piece is a great example of how a composer can create compelling music even with both hands playing in unison.

A Jealous Boy / *Être jaloux de son camarade qui a une grosse tête*
from Tiresome Pranks / *Peccadilles importunes*
Erik Satie

- Both hands are in five-finger position, though the L.H. sits between B and F, creating an unstable sound.
- The patterns in the L.H. are similar to accompaniment patterns in some music from the Classical era.
- The relentless pattern represents the slow burn of jealous feeling.
- Notice how throughout the piece, with the exception of m. 21-24, the R.H. and L.H. have the same phrase lengths.

Lullaby / *Berceuse*
from Picturesque Child's Play / *Enfantillages pittoresques*
Erik Satie

- This lullaby has a hypnotic quality, portraying the scene of Pierrot's mother putting him to bed.
- The hands remain in five-finger position throughout. However, this setup is higher on the keyboard, so you might need to move your seating position to the right.
- This piece is full of long phrases. At a slow tempo such as this, focus on slight *decrescendos* at the ends of phrases and giving new phrases a strong start.
- Both hands explore intervals of a third, fourth, and fifth. To become more comfortable with these, practice hands separately.
- Notice how in m. 29 to the end, Satie has both hands playing half notes to create a feeling of slowing down as the character Pierrot falls asleep.

Little Polka / *Petite Polka*
from I Play for Papa / *Je joue pour papa*
Alexandre Tansman

- The hands are very independent in this piece and should be practiced separately and slowly.
- This piece contains fingering issues for both hands, mostly in the form of large stretches.
- Try playing the R.H. notes in m. 1 as a single four-note chord. Then switch to the notes in m. 3 as a single chord. Feel whether your hand can rest comfortably on the chord or if you will have to use a rocking motion to reach notes.
- In the same way, practice the octave leaps in the L.H. in m. 13, 16, 32, 45, and 48.
- From m. 20 to 21, the L.H. thumb crosses slightly under the third finger to land on A.
- Since the first and third sections are exactly the same, we can call this musical structure ABA, a common form found in many different styles of music.
- The L.H. part seems to imitate a tuba, which would play the bass line in this type of music.
- This piece has a generally happy mood, as you would feel when dancing.

In the Fields / *Aux Champs*
from I Play for Papa / *Je joue pour papa*
Alexandre Tansman

- Play the R.H. in m. 1-4, then the L.H. in m. 9-12. Now try the L.H. in m. 1-4 and the R.H. in m. 9-12. You'll hear that they are exactly the same! The hands simply trade musical material between those two segments.
- In m. 9, note the instruction to "bring out the L.H.," since this is the melody.
- Practice hands separately and slowly.
- Make the most of the many *crescendos* followed by *decrescendos*.
- The overall character is a R.H. melody with L.H. accompaniment, except when they switch in m. 9-12.
- Tansman may have intended this piece to reflect contentment at some kind of activity or task outdoors.

Papa's Song / *Air Familier de Papa*
from I Play for Papa / *Je joue pour papa*
Alexandre Tansman

- This piece features two independent parts between the hands. Separate and slow practice is a must.
- As you practice slowly, also note the many hand position changes and finger crosses. It is important to enforce the correct fingering from the start.
- The many G-sharps in this piece hint that we are in the key of A minor.
- The form of this piece is essentially ABA, with just a slight difference between m. 5 and m. 21 (m. 1-8 = A, m. 9-16 = B, m. 17-24 = A).
- Pay close attention to all the *crescendos* and *decrescendos*. These dynamic changes help to shape the piece.
- The two independent voices create a texture of what we call counterpoint, evoking the spirit of J.S. Bach or other Baroque composers.

Taking advantage of corns on his feet to steal his hoop /
Profiter de ce qu'il a des cors aux pieds pour lui prendre son cerceau
from Tiresome Pranks / *Peccadilles importunes*
Erik Satie

- Satie was very whimsical and eccentric. The title is mysterious but here is an explanation: A thief has stolen a hoop from a boy with corns (small growths) on his feet that affect his ability to run. Satie's commentary within the piece refers to the thief.
- Both hands are in five-finger position.
- In m. 17-24, try not to accent the L.H.'s top C's too heavily. Focus on accenting the changing notes instead.
- Note the long phrases in the R.H., sometimes over four measures.
- Strive for an evenness of eighth notes, even when moving from hand to hand.

Octave Study / *Étude d'Octaves*
Olivier Hauray

- This is an exercise to strengthen your octave playing. If you have trouble stretching to reach an octave, this might help to increase your reach.
- Note that the first two pairs of notes are slurred, and followed by the phrase "*sim.*" or *simile*. This means to continue phrasing each two-note group the same way.
- The R.H. mostly goes up the octave, while the L.H. goes down.
- For variety, the composer briefly abandons octaves in m. 7-8 and m. 15-16.
- The pedal markings are the composer's.
- The marking "**D.C. al Fine**" at the end means to play from the beginning until the **Fine** in m. 8.
- This is a good example of how a composer can turn a simple technical exercise into compelling music.

Going Fishing / *À la Pêche*
from I Play for Papa / *Je joue pour papa*
Alexandre Tansman

- Tansman has given no articulations in this piece. How can we know if the notes should be light and bouncy or smooth and legato?
- We might suggest a slight separation between quarter notes, and *legato* eighth notes.
- Practice hands separately.
- The piece is essentially a R.H. melody with L.H. accompaniment.
- There are many dramatic changes of volume. For example, the dynamic changes from *mp* to *f* in just 4 bars from m. 10-13.
- Do not use any sustaining pedal in this piece.

Bear Cub / *L'Ourson*
from I Play for Papa / *Je joue pour papa*
Alexandre Tansman

- The R.H. always plays thirds or sixths (the inversion of a third).
- The L.H. primarily plays A and E.
- The changes from thirds to sixths in m. 13 and 15 might require some slow practice.
- In m. 18-20, try using some pedal to help the R.H. chord sustain to the end.
- Try to find a steady, quiet mood.

Mireille / *Mireille*
from Album for the Very Young, Op. 103 / *Album pour les tout-petits, Op. 103*
Mélanie Bonis

- Mireille is a French female name, suggesting that this piece is a portrait of a girl whom the composer knew.
- The R.H. part in m. 1-4 is a great exercise for finger independence. Practice it at different tempos but always steadily.
- Note the articulations in the L.H. in m. 3-4: *tenuto* followed by *staccato*. Work on a good contrast between the two.
- In m. 8-9, the running notes are briefly transferred to the L.H. Make sure these are just as smooth as in the R.H.
- The composer has created an interesting composition using a five-finger scale as some of the main material.

Sunset / *Soleil Couchant*
Olivier Hauray

- The opening expression *dolce e cantando* means "sweet and singing."
- Because the hands are interconnected, don't practice them separately; instead, work on locking into the rhythmic pattern between hands.
- If you divide up each measure as "1-and-2-and-3," the B in the L.H. of m. 1 comes on the "and" of beat 2.
- In m. 7-12, the pattern switches so that the R.H. now has eighth notes while the L.H. plays quarter notes.
- Note the finger crosses in the L.H. In m. 4-5 and 16-17, the L.H. second finger crosses over the thumb.

Bright Morning / *Clair Matin*
Olivier Hauray

- Note the key signature of G Major. All F's are sharp.
- This lively piece will sparkle if the articulations are properly observed. Practice a slight lift off of the ends of phrases.
- We have added dynamic markings to create contrast.
- Do not use any pedal in this piece.
- In m. 10, the opening motive is transferred to the L.H. Though the dynamic is marked as *f* for both hands, keep the L.H. slightly louder than the right.
- Also notice in m. 10 how the accompanying note in the R.H. occurs on the first beat of the L.H. phrase, instead of the second. This creates the feel of an offbeat.

Eating Bread and Butter / *Lui manger sa tartine*
from Tiresome Pranks / *Peccadilles importunes*
Erik Satie

- Satie was involved in the Dada movement, which celebrated absurdity and nonsense. This may explain some of his commentary in the piece.
- Both hands are in five-finger position: R.H. thumb on B above middle C, and L.H. thumb on A above middle C.
- Both hands alternate between playing *staccato* chords and *legato* lines. This piece is good training for mastering that "patting your head while rubbing your stomach" coordination.
- Aim for an even touch for the repeated chords that occur in both hands.

Meow! Purr! / *Miaou! Ronron!*
from Album for the Very Young, Op. 103 / *Album pour les tout-petits, Op. 103*
Mélanie Bonis

- Imagine a kitten gently walking on the piano keys.
- This piece explores the topic of half-steps and chromatic scales. Read the sharps, flats and naturals carefully as you work through the winding lines in m. 3-4 and m. 8-13.
- Don't try to play softly until you have mastered the piece. At that point, observe ***pppp***, which is the composer's way of saying, "play as softly as possible."
- There are musical challenges, such as m. 13, where the composer asks for a swell of volume and a slowing down, followed by a return to the opening tempo and a sudden shift to ***p*** on the downbeat of m. 14.
- The composer's indication of *lié* at the opening means "connected", and probably implies using sustaining pedal.

In the Garden / *Au jardin*
from For Children, Volume 2 / *Pour les enfants, volume 2*
Alexandre Tansman

- The L.H. has an accompaniment pattern with the first note on the "and" of beat 1. Don't overly accent the first note.
- The composer has given no articulations, so you can make choices about how to articulate and phrase the music.
- Throughout, the R.H. has the melody while the L.H. serves as accompaniment.
- The last four bars feature a large hand position change. Practice moving the L.H. thumb down to the low A in m. 21, and then up to D in m. 22, and back down to A in m. 24.

The Sweet Little Girl / *La gentille toute petite Fille*
Three New Children's Pieces / *Trois nouvelles Enfantines*
Erik Satie

- Note the long phrases in both hands.
- In m. 13-14, the bottom notes in the treble staff are taken with the L.H. In m. 22, the top notes in the bass staff are taken with the R.H.
- The continuous L.H. eighth note line may seem overwhelming, but it is easier to follow if you circle the notes that occur on the strong beats. For example, in m. 1, circle the F and the E.
- Keep the eighth notes steady and even.

The Naughty Boy / *Le vilain petit Vaurien*
Three New Children's Pieces / *Trois nouvelles Enfantines*
Erik Satie

- The two hands sometimes share the same staff in this piece. Note the markings of l.h. and r.h., as well as the bracket symbols, which designate the notes each hand plays.
- There are many hand position changes between phrases. Try a slight lift between phrases to set your hand in the next position.
- The repeated *staccato* eighth notes in m. 5-6, 11-12, and 21-24 all occur during text about the boy laughing. Perhaps this is a musical portrayal of his laugh.
- There is a playful quality in this piece, with the hands jumping between staves in the dialogue between the mother and the naughty boy.

– Brendan Fox
editor

Little Prelude to the Day

from *Picturesque Child's Play*

Erik Satie

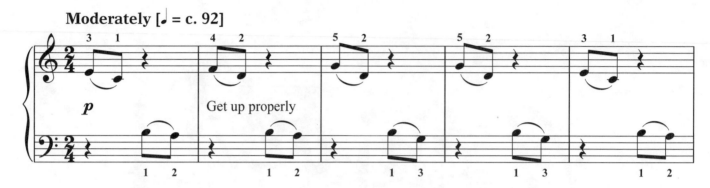

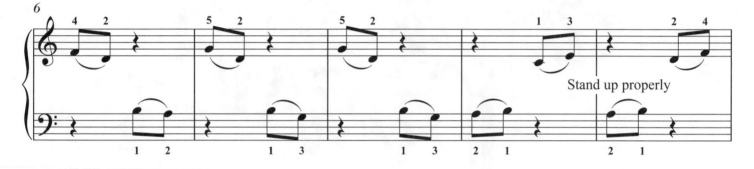

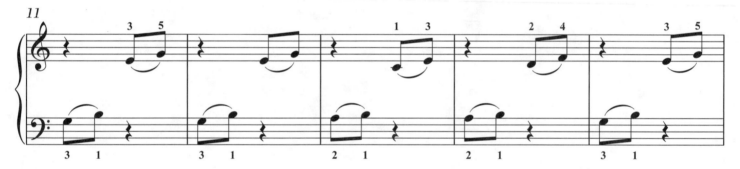

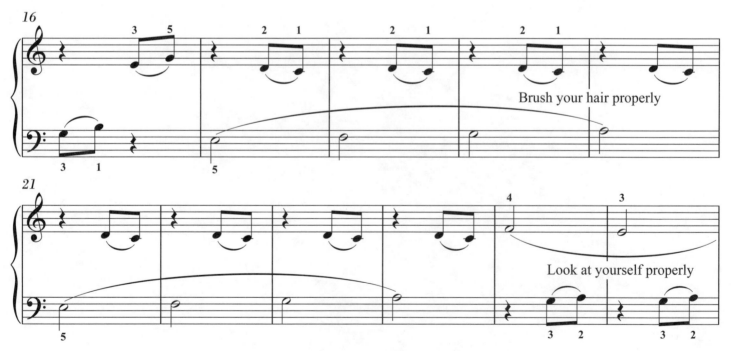

Satie often included phrases of narrative text in his piano music. He forbade these to be read aloud during performance.

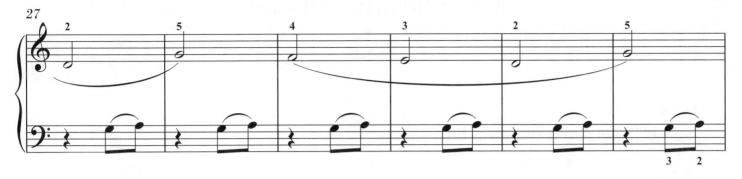

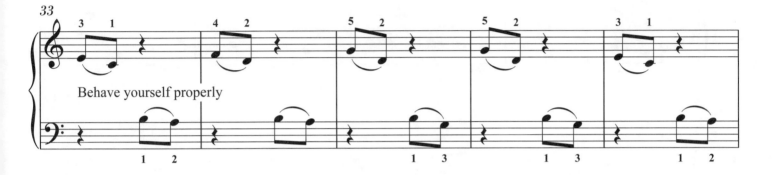

Behave yourself properly

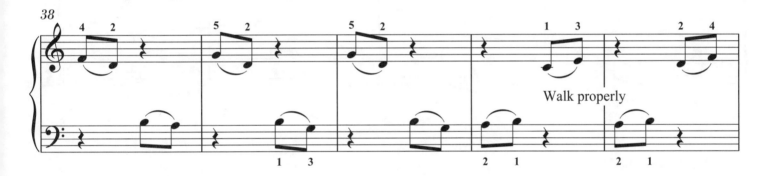

Walk properly

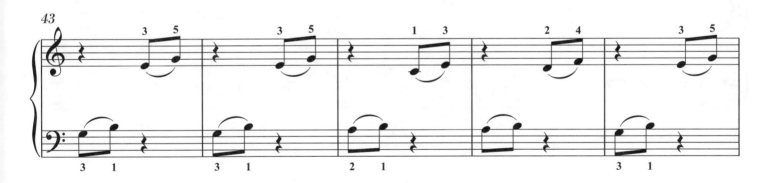

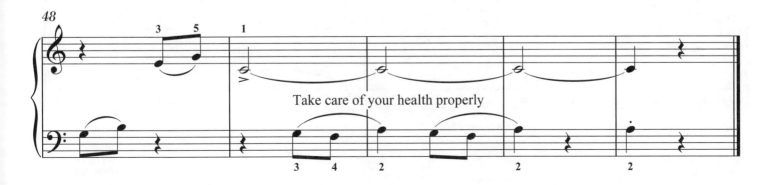

Take care of your health properly

Melodies in Octaves

Olivier Hauray

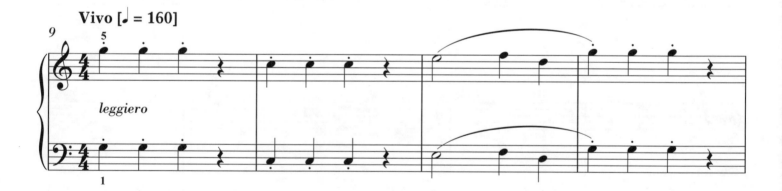

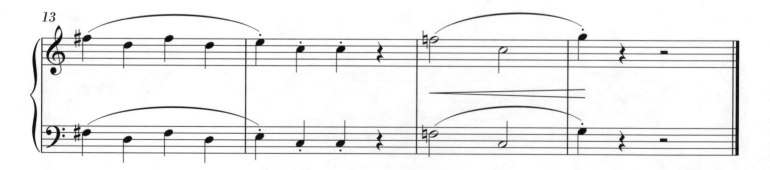

A Jealous Boy

from *Tiresome Pranks*

Erik Satie

A jealous person is not a happy person

I once knew a little boy who was · jealous of his parrot.

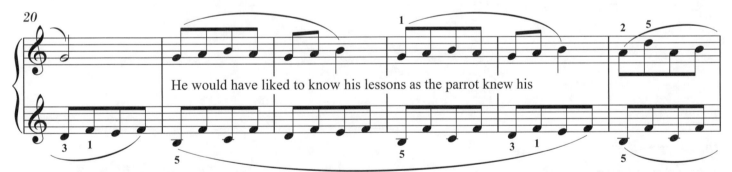

He would have liked to know his lessons as the parrot knew his

Slow down

Satie often included phrases of narrative text in his piano music. He forbade these to be read aloud during performance.

Lullaby

from *Picturesque Child's Play*

Erik Satie

Satie often included phrases of narrative text in his piano music. He forbade these to be read aloud during performance.

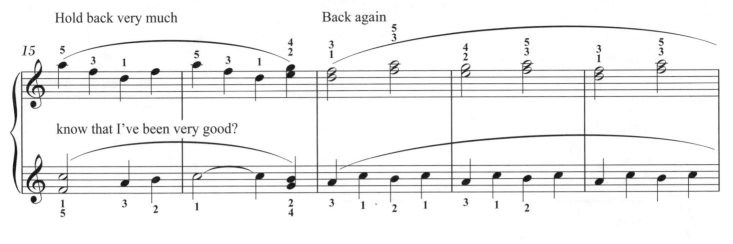

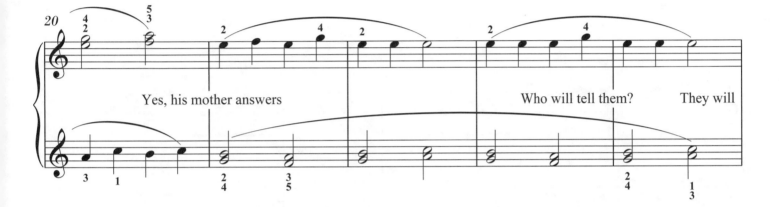

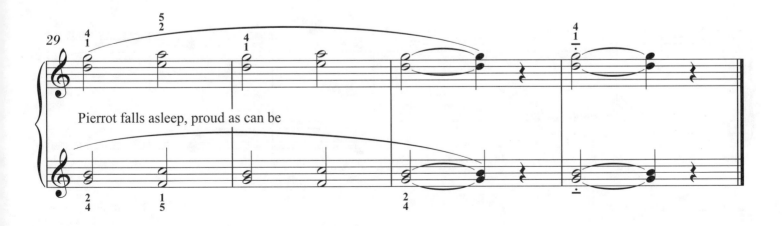

Little Polka
from *I Play for Papa*

Alexandre Tansman

Lively [♩ = 120–130]

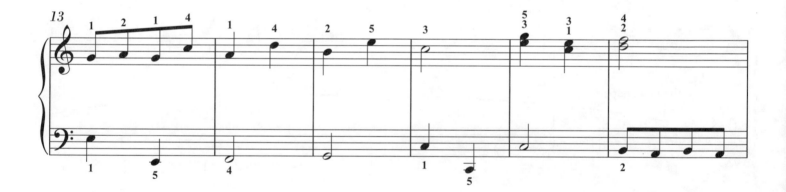

Tous droits réservés
pour tous pays

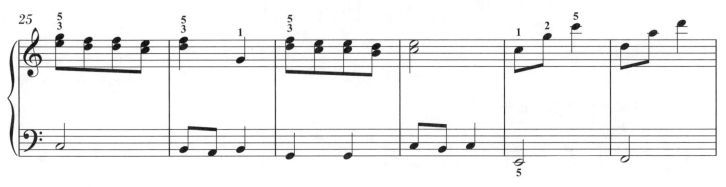

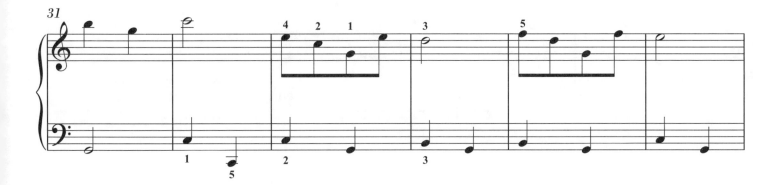

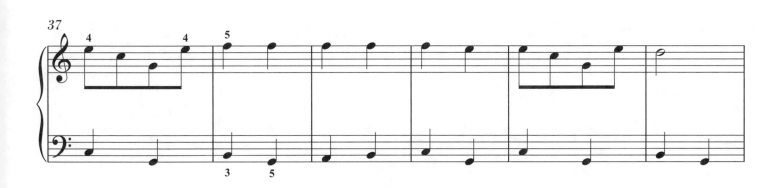

In the Fields

from *I Play for Papa*

Alexandre Tansman

Papa's Song

from *I Play for Papa*

Alexandre Tansman

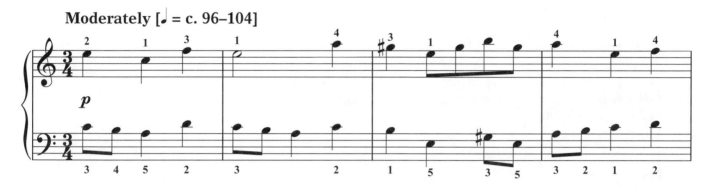

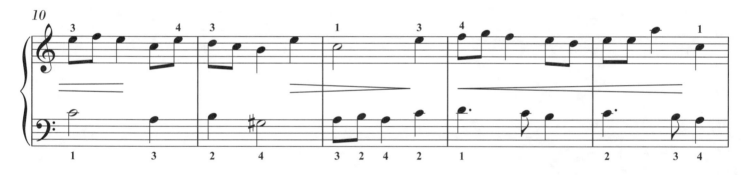

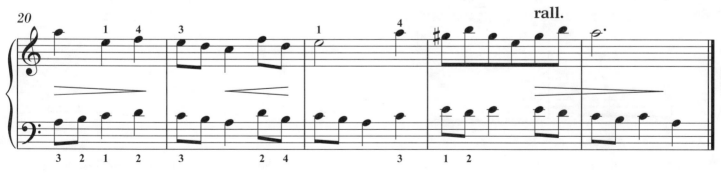

Taking advantage of the corns on his feet to steal his hoop

from *Tiresome Pranks*

Erik Satie

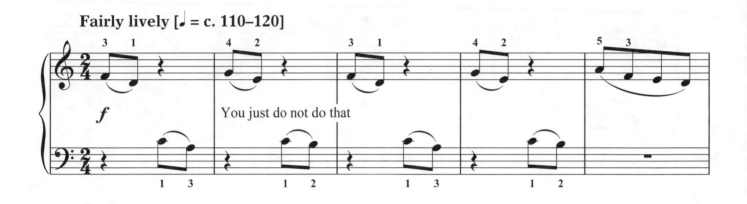

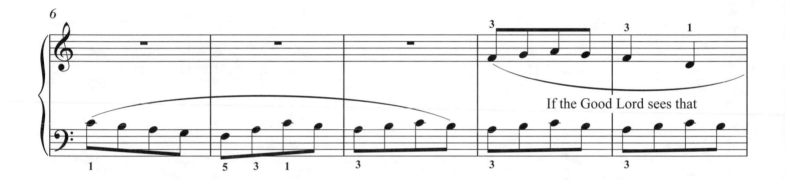

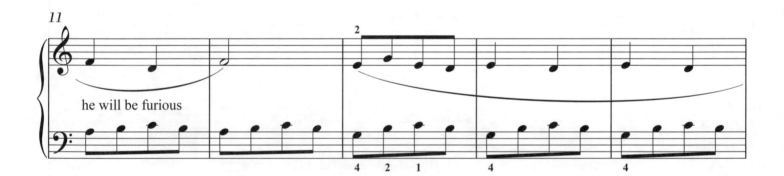

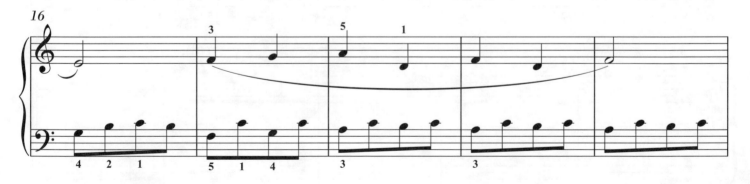

Satie often included phrases of narrative text in his piano music. He forbade these to be read aloud during performance.

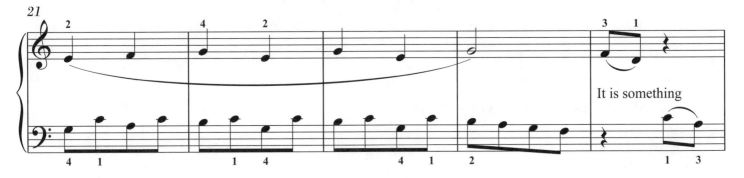

It is something

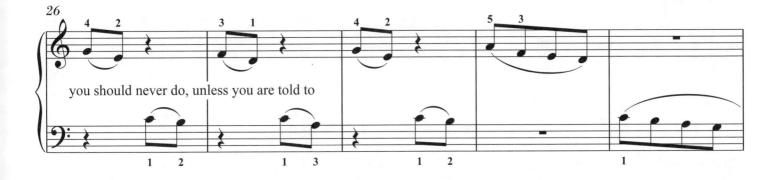

you should never do, unless you are told to

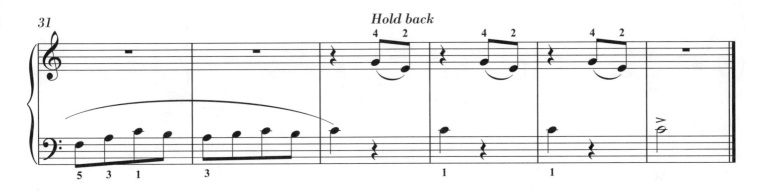

Octave Study

Olivier Hauray

Going Fishing

from *I Play for Papa*

Alexandre Tansman

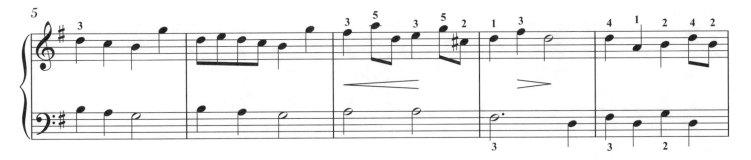

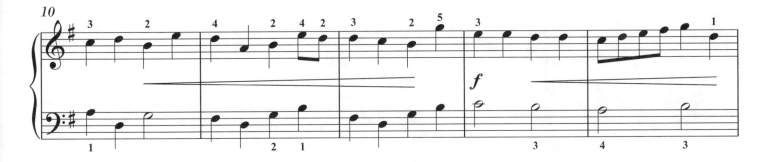

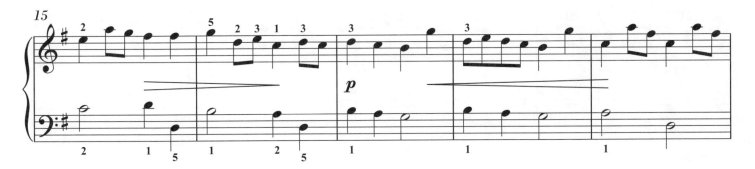

Bear Cub

from *I Play for Papa*

Alexandre Tansman

Moderately [♩ = c. 90–96]

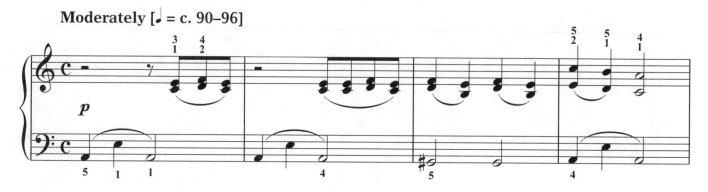

Mireille

from *Album for the Very Young,* Op. 103

Mélanie Bonis

Sunset

Olivier Hauray

[**Andantino** ♩ = c. 76–80]
dolce e cantando

Bright Morning

Olivier Hauray

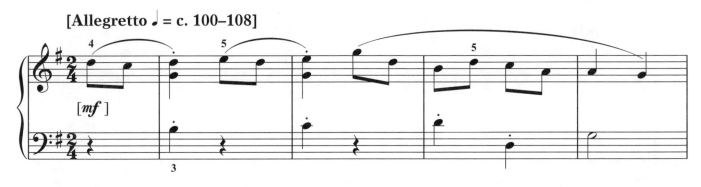

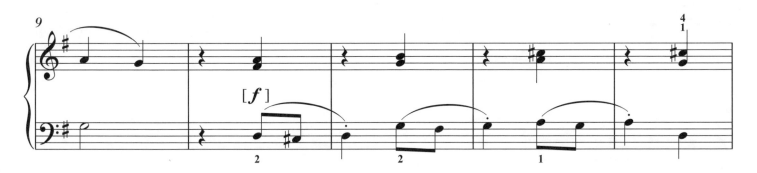

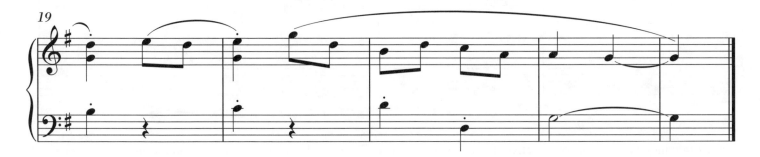

Eating Bread and Butter

from *Tiresome Pranks*

Erik Satie

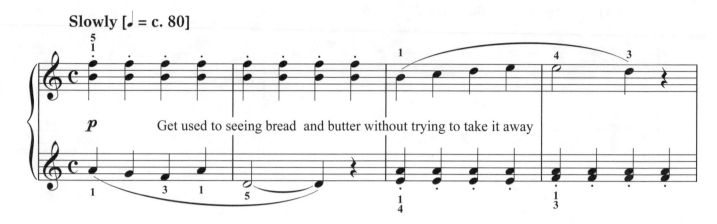

Slowly [♩ = c. 80]

p Get used to seeing bread and butter without trying to take it away

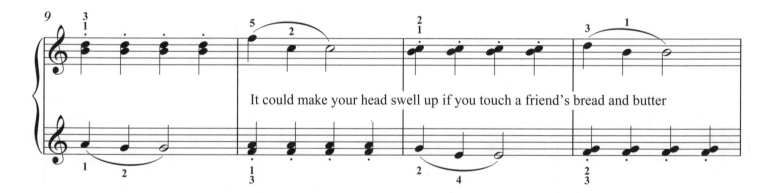

It could make your head swell up if you touch a friend's bread and butter

Hold back very much and decrease

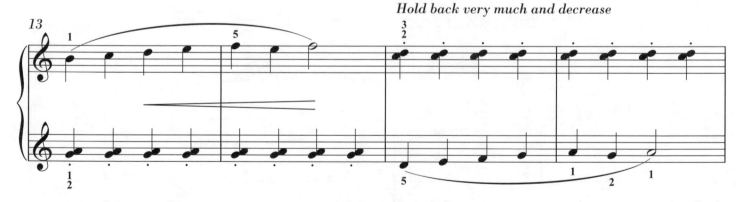

Satie often included phrases of narrative text in his piano music. He forbade these to be read aloud during performance.

I had a dog who secretly smoked all my cigars

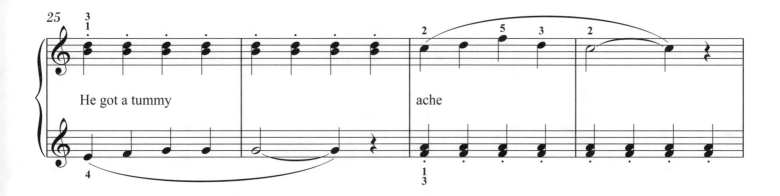

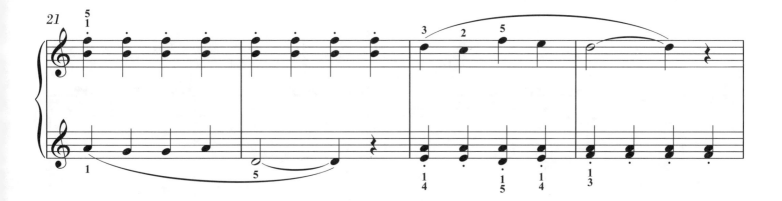

He got a tummy ache

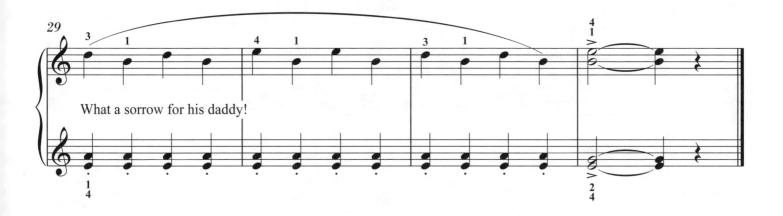

What a sorrow for his daddy!

Meow! Purr!

from *Album for the Very Young*, Op. 103

Mélanie Bonis

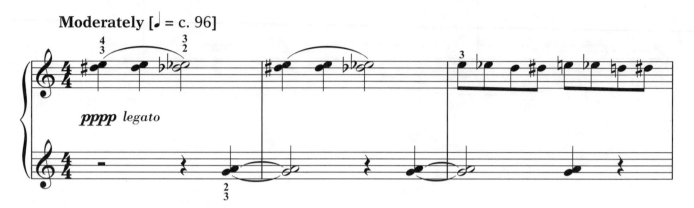

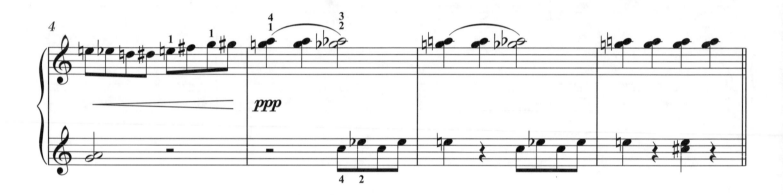

Fingerings are by the composer.

In the Garden

from *For Children*, Volume 2

Alexandre Tansman

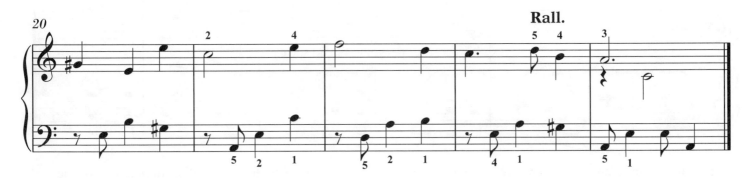

The Sweet Little Girl

from *Three New Children's Pieces*

Erik Satie

Satie often included phrases of narrative text in his piano music. He forbade these to be read aloud during performance.

The Naughty Boy

from *Three New Children's Pieces*

Erik Satie

Dynamics, fingerings and tempo are editorial suggestions.

Satie often included phrases of narrative text in his piano music. He forbade these to be read aloud during performance.